THE
WHEEL

Wendell Berry

North Point Press
San Francisco
1982

Some of the poems in this volume first appeared in the following magazines: *Apple, The Georgia Review, Harvard Magazine, The Kentucky Poetry Review, Kuksu, The Ontario Review, The Sewanee Review, The Southern Review.*

"Desolation," "From the Distance," "The Law That Marries All Things," "The River Bridged and Forgot," "Setting Out," "Song," and "The Strait" first appeared in *The Hudson Review.*

"My Children, Coming of Age" and "The Dance" were first published in the *Sewanee Review* 84 (Summer 1976).

A few of these poems appeared in chapbooks published by the following small presses: The Deerfield Press (THE GIFT OF GRAVITY); Sand Dollar (THREE MEMORIAL POEMS).

It needs a more refined perception to recognize throughout this stupendous wealth of varying shapes and forms the principle of stability. Yet this principle dominates. It dominates by means of an ever-recurring cycle . . . repeating itself silently and ceaselessly. . . . This cycle is constituted of the successive and repeated processes of birth, growth, maturity, death, and decay.

An eastern religion calls this cycle the Wheel of Life and no better name could be given to it. The revolutions of this Wheel never falter and are perfect. Death supersedes life and life rises again from what is dead and decayed.

Sir Albert Howard,
The Soil and Health: A Study of Organic Agriculture

Contents

V

VI

*Owen Flood / January 13, 1920–**March** 27, 1974* I

Requiem

1.

We will see no more
the mown grass fallen behind him
on the still ridges before night,
or hear him laughing in the crop rows,
or know the order of his delight.

Though the green fields are my delight,
elegy is my fate. I have come to be
survivor of many and of much
that I love, that I won't live to see
come again into this world.

Things that mattered to me once
won't matter any more,
for I have left the safe shore
where magnificence of art
could suffice my heart.

2.

In the day of his work
when the grace of the world
was upon him, he made his way,
not turning back or looking aside,
light in his stride.

Now may the grace of death
be upon him, his spirit blessed
in deep song of the world
and the stars turning, the seasons
returning, and long rest.

Elegy

1.

To be at home on its native ground
the mind must go down below its horizon,
descend below the lightfall
on ridge and steep and valley floor
to receive the lives of the dead. It must wake
in their sleep, who wake in its dreams.

"Who is here?" On the rock road between
creek and woods in the fall of the year,
I stood and listened. I heard the cries
of little birds high in the wind.
And then the beat of old footsteps
came around me, and my sight was changed.

I passed through the lens of darkness
as though a furrow, and the dead
gathered to meet me. They knew me,
but looked in wonder at the lines in my face,
the white hairs sprinkled on my head.

I saw a tall old man leaning
upon a cane, his open hand
raised in some fierce commendation,
knowledge of long labor in his eyes;
another, a gentler countenance,
smiling beneath a brim of sweaty felt
in welcome to me as before.

I saw an old woman, a saver
of little things, whose lonely grief
was the first I knew; and one bent
with age and pain, whose busy hands
worked out a selflessness of love.

Those were my teachers. And there were more,
beloved of face and name, who once bore
the substance of our common ground.
Their eyes, having grieved all grief, were clear.

2.

I saw one standing aside, alone,
weariness in his shoulders, his eyes
bewildered yet with the newness
of his death. In my sorrow I felt,
as many times before, gladness
at the sight of him. "Owen," I said.

He turned—lifted, tilted his hand.
I handed him a clod of earth
picked up in a certain well-known field.
He kneaded it in his palm and spoke:
"Wendell, this is not a place
for you and me." And then he grinned;
we recognized his stubborness—
it was his principle to doubt
all ease of satisfaction.

"The crops are in the barn," I said,
"the morning frost has come to the fields,
and I have turned back to accept,
if I can, what none of us could prevent."

He stood, remembering, weighing the cost
of the division we had come to,
his fingers resting on the earth
he held cupped lightly in his palm.
It seemed to me then that he cast off
his own confusion, and assumed
for one last time, in one last kindness,
the duty of the older man.

He nodded his head. "The desire I had
in early morning and in spring,
I never wore it out. I had
the desire, if I had had the strength.
But listen—what we prepared
to have, we have."

He raised his eyes.
"Look," he said.

3.

We stood on a height,
woods above us, and below
on the half-mowed slope we saw ourselves
as we were once: a young man mowing,
a boy grubbing with an axe.

It was an old abandoned field,
long overgrown with thorns and briars.
We made it new in the heat haze
of that midsummer: he, proud
of the ground intelligence clarified,
and I, proud in his praise.

"I wish," I said, "that we could be
back in that good time again."

"We are back there again, today
and always. Where else would we be?"
He smiled, looked at me, and I knew
it was my mind he led me through.
He spoke of some infinitude
of thought.

             He led me to another
slope beside another woods,
this lighted only by stars. Older
now, the man and the boy lay
on their backs in deep grass, quietly
talking. In the distance moved
the outcry of one deep-voiced hound.

Other voices joined that voice:
another place, a later time,
a hunter's fire among the trees,
faces turned to the blaze, laughter
and then silence, while in the dark
around us lay long breaths of sleep.

4.
And then, one by one, he moved me
through all the fields of our lives,
preparations, plantings, harvests,
crews joking at the row ends,
the water jug passing like a kiss.

He spoke of our history passing through us,
the way our families' generations
overlap, the great teaching
coming down by deed of companionship:
characters of fields and times and men,
qualities of devotion and of work—
endless fascinations, passions
old as mind, new as light.

All our years around us, near us,
I saw him furious and narrow,
like most men, and saw the virtue
that made him unlike most.
It was his passion to be true
to the condition of the Fall—
to live by the sweat of his face, to eat
his bread, assured that cost was paid.

5.
We came then to his time of pain,
when the early morning light showed,
as always, the sweet world, and all
an able, well-intentioned man

might do by dark, and his strength failed
before the light. His body had begun
too soon its earthward journey,
filling with gravity, and yet his mind
kept its old way.

                    Again, in the sun
of his last harvest, I heard him say:
"Do you want to take this row,
and let me get out of your way?"
I saw the world ahead of him then
for the first time, and I saw it
as he already had seen it,
himself gone from it. It was a sight
I could not see and not weep.
He reached and would have touched me
with his hand, though he could not.

    6.
Finally, he brought me to a hill
overlooking the fields that once
belonged to him, that he once
belonged to. "Look," he said again.
I knew he wanted me to see
the years of care that place wore,
for his story lay upon it, a bloom,
a blessing.

                    The time and place so near,
we almost *were* the men we watched.

Summer's end sang in the light.
We spoke of death and obligation,
the limits of both things and men.
Words never moved so heavily
between us, or cost us more. We hushed.
And then that man who bore his death
in him, and knew it, quietly said:
"Well. It's a fascinating world,
after all."

His life so powerfully
stood there in presence of his place
and work and time, I could not
realize except with grief
that only his spirit now was with me.

In the very hour he died, I told him,
before I knew his death, the thought
of years to come had moved me
like a call. I thought of healing,
health, friendship going on,
the generations gathering, our good times
reaching one best time of all.

7.

My mind was overborne with questions
I could not speak. It seemed to me
we had returned now to the dark
valley where our journey began.
But a brightening intelligence

was on his face. Insight moved him
as he once was moved by daylight.

The best teachers teach more
than they know. By their deaths
they teach most. They lead us beyond
what we know, and what they knew.
Thus my teacher, my old friend,
stood smiling now before me, wholly
moved by what had moved him partly
in the world.

            Again the host of the dead
encircled us, as in a dance.
And I was aware now of the unborn
moving among them. As they turned
I could see their bodies come to light
and fade again in the dark throng.
They moved as to a distant or a hovering
song I strained for, but could not hear.

"Our way is endless," my teacher said.
"The Creator is divided in Creation
for the joys of recognition. We knew
that Spirit in each other once;
it brings us here. By its divisions
and returns, the world lives.
Both mind and earth are made
of what its light gives and uses up.
So joy contains, survives its cost.

The dead abide, as grief knows.
We are what we have lost."

There is a song in the Creation;
it has always been the gift
of every gifted voice, though none
ever sang it. As he spoke
I heard that song. In its changes and returns
his life was passing into life.
That moment, earth and song and mind,
the living and the dead, were one.

8.

At last, completed in his rest,
as one who has worked and bathed, fed
and loved and slept, he let fall
the beloved earth that I had brought him.
He raised his hand, turned me to my way.
And I, inheritor of what I mourned,
went back toward the light of day.

Rising

for Kevin Flood

1.

Having danced until nearly
time to get up, I went on
in the harvest, half lame
with weariness. And he
took no notice, and made
no mention of my distress.
He went ahead, assuming
that I would follow. I followed,
dizzy, half blind, bitter
with sweat in the hot light.
He never turned his head,
a man well known by his back
in those fields in those days.
He led me through long rows
of misery, moving like a dancer
ahead of me, so elated
he was, and able, filled
with desire for the ground's growth.
We came finally to the high
still heat of four o'clock,
a long time before sleep.
And then he stood by me
and looked at me as I worked,
just looked, so that my own head
uttered his judgment, even

his laughter. He only said:
"That social life don't get
down the row, does it, boy?"

2.

I worked by will then, he
by desire. What was ordeal
for me, for him was order
and grace, ideal and real.

That was my awkward boyhood,
the time of his mastery.
He troubled me to become
what I had not thought to be.

3.

The boy must learn the man
whose life does not travel
along any road, toward
any other place,
but is a journey back and forth
in rows, and in the rounds
of years. His journey's end
is no place of ease, but the farm
itself, the place day labor
starts from, journeys in,
returns to: the fields
whose past and potency are one.

4.

And that is our story,
not of time, but the forever
returning events of light,
ancient knowledge seeking
its new minds. The man at dawn
in spring of the year,
going to the fields,
visionary of seed and desire,
is timeless as a star.

5.

Any man's death could end the story:
his mourners, having accompanied him
to the grave through all he knew,
turn back, leaving him complete.

But this is not the story of a life.
It is the story of lives, knit together,
overlapping in succession, rising
again from grave after grave.

For those who depart from it, bearing it
in their minds, the grave is a beginning.
It has weighted the earth with sudden
new gravity, the enrichment of pain.

There is a grave, too, in each
survivor. By it, the dead one lives.

He enters us, a broken blade,
sharp, clear as a lens or a mirror.

And he comes into us helpless, tender
as the newborn enter the world. Great
is the burden of our care. We must be true
to ourselves. How else will he know us?

Like a wound, grief receives him.
Like graves, we heal over, and yet keep
as part of ourselves the severe gift.
By grief, more inward than darkness,

the dead become the intelligence of life.
Where the tree falls the forest rises.
There is nowhere to stand but in absence,
no life but in the fateful light.

6.

Ended, a story is history;
it is in time, with time
lost. But if a man's life
continue in another man,
then the flesh will rhyme
its part in immortal song.
By absence, he comes again.

There is a kinship of the fields
that gives to the living the breath
of the dead. The earth

opened in the spring, opens
in all springs. Nameless,
ancient, many-lived, we reach
through ages with the seed.

II

Desolation

A gracious Spirit sings as it comes
and goes. It moves forever
among things. Earth and flesh, passing
into each other, sing together.

Turned against that song, we go
where no singing is or light
or need coupled with its yes,
but spite, despair, fear, and loneliness.

Unless the solitary will forbear,
time enters the flesh to sever
passion from all care,
annul the lineage of consequence.

Unless the solitary will forbear,
the blade enters the ground
to tear the world's comfort
out, by root and crown.

The Strait

The valley holds its shadow.
My loves lie round me in the dark.
Through the woods on the hilltop
I see one distant light, a star
that seems to sway and flicker
as the trees move. I see the flight
of men crossing and crossing
the blank curve of heaven. I hear
the branches clashing in the wind.

2.

I have come to the end
of what I have supposed,
following my thread of song.
Who knows where it is going?

I am well-acquainted now
among the dead. Only the past
knows me. In solitude
who will teach me?

3.

The world's one song is passing
in and out of deaths, as thrush notes
move in the shadows, nearer and nearer,

and then away, intent, in the hollows
of the woods. It does not attend
the dead, or what will die. It is light
though it goes in the dark. It goes
ahead, summoning. What hears follows.

4.

Sitting among the bluebells
in my sorrow, for lost time
and the never forgotten dead,
I saw a hummingbird stand
in air to drink from flowers.
It was a kiss he took and gave.
At his lightness and the ardor
of his throat, the song I live by
stirred my mind. I said:
"By sweetness alone it survives."

The Law That Marries All Things

1.
The cloud is free only
to go with the wind.

The rain is free
only in falling.

The water is free only
in its gathering together,

in its downward courses,
in its rising into air.

2.
In law is rest
if you love the law,
if you enter, singing, into it
as water in its descent.

3.
Or song is truest law,
and you must enter singing;
it has no other entrance.

It is the great chorus
of parts. The only outlawry
is in division.

4.
Whatever is singing
is found, awaiting the return
of whatever is lost.

5.
Meet us in the air
over the water,
sing the swallows.

Meet me, meet me,
the redbird sings,
here here here here.

Setting Out

for Gurney Norman

Even love must pass through loneliness,
the husbandman become again
the Long Hunter, and set out
not to the familiar woods of home
but to the forest of the night,
the true wilderness, where renewal
is found, the lay of the ground
a premonition of the unknown.
Blowing leaf and flying wren
lead him on. He can no longer be at home,
he cannot return, unless he begin
the circle that first will carry him away.

Song (1)

In ignorance of the source, our want
affirms abundance in these days.
Truth keeps us though we do not know it.
O Spirit, our desolation is your praise.

From the Distance

1.
We are others and the earth,
the living of the dead.
Remembering who we are,
we live in eternity;
any solitary act
is work of community.

2.
All times are one
if heart delight
in work, if hands
join the world right.

3.
The wheel of eternity is turning
in time, its rhymes, austere,
at long intervals returning,
sing in the mind, not in the ear.

4.
A man of faithful thought may feel
in light, among the beasts and fields,
the turning of the wheel.

Letter

1.

To search for what belongs where it is,
for what, scattered, might come together,
I leave you, my mold, my cup;
I flow from your bonds, a stream risen
over the hold of its stones.

2.

Turning always in my mind toward you,
your slopes, folds, gentle openings
on which I would rest my song
like an open hand, I know the trials of absence,
comely lives I must pass by, not to return,
beauties I will not know in satisfaction,
but in the sharp clarity of desire.

3.

In place with you, as I come and go
I pass the thread of my song again
and again through the web of my life
and the lives of the dead before me,
the old resounding in the new.
Now in the long curve of a journey
I spin a single strand, carried away
by what must bring me home.

Returning

I was walking in a dark valley
and above me the tops of the hills
had caught the morning light.
I heard the light singing as it went out
among the grassblades and the leaves.
I waded upward through the shadow
until my head emerged,
my shoulders were mantled with the light,
and my whole body came up
out of the darkness, and stood
on the new shore of the day.
Where I had come was home,
for my own house stood white
where the dark river wore the earth.
The sheen of bounty was on the grass,
and the spring of the year had come.

To Tanya at Christmas

Forgive me, my delight,
that grief and loneliness
have kept me. Though I come
to you in darkness, you are
companion of the light
that rises on all I know.

In the long night of the year
and of the spirit, God's birth
is met with simple noise.
Deaf and blind in division,
I reach, and do not find.
You show the gentler way:
We come to good by love;
our words must be made flesh.

And flesh must be made word
at last, our lives rise
in speech to our children's tongues.
They will tell how we once stood
together here, two trees
whose lives in annual sheddings
made their way into this ground,
whose bodies turned to earth
and song. The song will tell
how old love sweetens the fields.

Song (2)

My gentle hill, I rest
beside you in the dark
in a place warmed by my body,
where by ardor, grace, work,
and loss, I belong.

IV

The River Bridged and Forgot

Who can impair thee, mighty King

Bridged and forgot, the river
in unwearying descent
carries down the soil
of ravaged uplands, waste
and acid from the stripmines,
poisons of our false
prosperity. What mind
regains of clarity
mourns, the current a slow
cortege of everything
that we have given up,
the materials of Creation
wrecked, the strewed substance
of our trust and dignity.

But on still afternoons
of summer, the water's face
recovers clouds, the shapes
of leaves. Maple, willow,
sycamore stand light
and easy in their weight,
their branching forms formed
on the water, and yellow
warbler, swallow, oriole
stroke their deft flight
through the river's serene reflection
of the sky, as though, corrupted,

it shows the incorrupt.
Is this memory or promise?

And what is grief beside it?
What is anger beside it?
It is unfinished. It will not
be finished. And a man's life
will be, although his work
will not, nor his desire
for clarity. Beside
this dark passage of water
I make my work, life work
of many lives that has
no end, for it takes circles
of years, of birth and death
for pattern, eternal form
visible in mystery.
It takes for pattern the heavenly
and earthly song of which
it is a part, which holds it
from despair: the joined voices
of all things, all muteness
vocal in their harmony.
For that, though none can hear
or sing it all, though I
must by nature fail,
my work has turned away

the priced infinity
of mechanical desire.

This work that many loves
inspire teaches the mind
resemblance to the earth
in seasonal fashioning,
departures and returns
of song. The hands strive
against their gravity
for envisioned lights and forms,
fallings of harmony;
they strive, fail at their season's
end. The seasonless river
lays hand and handiwork
upon the world, obedient
to a greater mind, whole
past holding or beholding,
in whose flexing signature
all the dooms assemble
and become the lives of things.

The Gift of Gravity

All that passes descends,
and ascends again unseen
into the light: the river
coming down from sky
to hills, from hills to sea,
and carving as it moves,
to rise invisible,
gathered to light, to return
again. "The river's injury
is its shape." I've learned no more.
We are what we are given
and what is taken away;
blessed be the name
of the giver and taker.
For everything that comes
is a gift, the meaning always
carried out of sight
to renew our whereabouts,
always a starting place.
And every gift is perfect
in its beginning, for it
is "from above, and cometh down
from the Father of lights."
Gravity is grace.
All that has come to us
has come as the river comes,
given in passing away.

And if our wickedness
destroys the watershed,
dissolves the beautiful field,
then I must grieve and learn
that I possess by loss
the earth I live upon
and stand in and am. The dark
and then the light will have it.
I am newborn of pain
to love the new-shaped shore
where young cottonwoods
take hold and thrive in the wound,
kingfishers already nesting
in a hole in the sheared bank.
"What is left is what is"—
have learned no more. The shore
turns green under the songs
of the fires of the world's end,
and what is there to do?
Imagine what exists
so that it may shine
in thought light and day light,
lifted up in the mind.
The dark returns to light
in the kingfisher's blue and white
richly laid together.
He falls into flight
from the broken ground,
with strident outcry gathers
air under his wings.
In work of love, the body

forgets its weight. And once
again with love and singing
in mind, I come to what
must come to me, carried
as a dancer by a song.
This grace is gravity.

V

Song (3)

I stood and heard the steps of the city
and dreamed a lighter stepping than I heard,
the tread of my people dancing in a ring.
I knew that circle broken, the steps awry,
stone and iron humming in the air.

But I thought even there, among the straying
steps, of the dance that circles life around,
its shadows moving on the ground, in rhyme
of flesh with flesh, time with time, our bliss,
the earthly song that heavenly is.

The Wheel

for Robert Penn Warren

At the first strokes of the fiddle bow
the dancers rise from their seats.
The dance begins to shape itself
in the crowd, as couples join,
and couples join couples, their movement
together lightening their feet.
They move in the ancient circle
of the dance. The dance and the song
call each other into being. Soon
they are one—rapt in a single
rapture, so that even the night
has its clarity, and time
is the wheel that brings it round.

In this rapture the dead return.
Sorrow is gone from them.
They are light. They step
into the steps of the living
and turn with them in the dance
in the sweet enclosure
of the song, and timeless
is the wheel that brings it round.

The Dance

I would have each couple turn,
join and unjoin, be lost
in the greater turning
of other couples, woven
in the circle of a dance,
the song of long time flowing

over them, so they may return,
turn again in to themselves
out of desire greater than their own,
belonging to all, to each,
to the dance, and to the song
that moves them through the night.

What is fidelity? To what
does it hold? The point
of departure, or the turning road
that is departure and absence
and the way home? What we are
and what we were once

are far estranged. For those
who would not change, time
is infidelity. But we are married
until death, and are betrothed
to change. By silence, so,
I learn my song. I earn

my sunny fields by absence, once
and to come. And I love you
as I love the dance that brings you
out of the multitude
in which you come and go.
Love changes, and in change is true.

Passing the Strait

1.

Forsaking all others, we
are true to all. What we love
here, we would not desecrate
anywhere. Seed or song, work
or sleep, no matter the need,
what we let fall, we keep.

2.

The dance passes beyond us,
our loves loving their loves,
and returns, having passed through
the breaths and sleeps of the world,
the woven circuits of desire,
which leaving here arrive here.
Love moves in a bright sphere.

3.

Past the strait of kept faith
the flesh rises, is joined
to light. Risen from distraction
and weariness, we come
into the turning and changing
circle of all lovers. On this height
our labor changes into flight.

Our Children, Coming of Age

In the great circle, dancing in
and out of time, you move now
toward your partners, answering
the music suddenly audible to you
that only carried you before
and will carry you again.
When you meet the destined ones
now dancing toward you,
we will be in line behind you,
out of your awareness for the time,
we whom you know, others we remember
whom you do not remember, others
forgotten by us all.
When you meet, and hold love
in your arms, regardless of all,
the unknown will dance away from you
toward the horizon of light.
Our names will flutter
on these hills like little fires.

Song (4)

for Guy Davenport

Within the circles of our lives
we dance the circles of the years,
the circles of the seasons
within the circles of the years,
the cycles of the moon
within the circles of the seasons,
the circles of our reasons
within the cycles of the moon.

Again, again we come and go,
changed, changing. Hands
join, unjoin in love and fear,
grief and joy. The circles turn,
each giving into each, into all,
Only music keeps us here,

each by all the others held.
In the hold of hands and eyes
we turn in pairs, that joining
joining each to all again.

And then we turn aside, alone,
out of the sunlight gone

into the darker circles of return.

VI

In Rain

1.
I go in under foliage
light with rain-light
in the hill's cleft,
and climb, my steps
silent as flight
on the wet leaves.
Where I go, stones
are wearing away
under the sky's flow.

2.

The path I follow
I can hardly see
it is so faintly trod
and over grown.
At times, looking,
I fail to find it
among dark trunks, leaves
living and dead. And then
I am alone, the woods
shapeless around me.
I look away, my gaze
at rest among leaves,
and then I see the path
again, a dark way going on
through the light.

3.

In a mist of light
falling with the rain
I walk this ground
of which dead men
and women I have loved
are part, as they
are part of me. In earth,
in blood, in mind,
the dead and living
into each other pass,
as the living pass
in and out of loves
as stepping to a song.
The way I go is
marriage to this place,
grace beyond chance,
love's braided dance
covering the world.

4.

Marriages to marriages
are joined, husband and wife
are plighted to all
husbands and wives,
any life has all lives
for its delight.
Let the rain come,
the sun, and then the dark,
for I will rest
in an easy bed tonight.

Design by David Bullen
Typeset in Mergenthaler Sabon
by Wilsted & Taylor
Printed by Bookcrafters
on acid-free paper